Where the World Is Made

The Katharine Bakeless Nason Literary Publication Prizes

The Bakeless Literary Publication Prizes are sponsored by the Bread Loaf Writers' Conference of Middlebury College to support the publication of first books. The manuscripts are selected through an open competition and are published by University Press of New England/Middlebury College Press.

Competition Winners in Poetry

1996
Mary Jo Bang, *Apology for Want*
JUDGE: Edward Hirsch

1997
m loncar, *66 galaxie*
JUDGE: Garret Hongo

1998
Chris Forhan, *Forgive Us Our Happiness*
Daniel Tobin, *Where the World Is Made*
JUDGE: Ellen Bryant Voigt

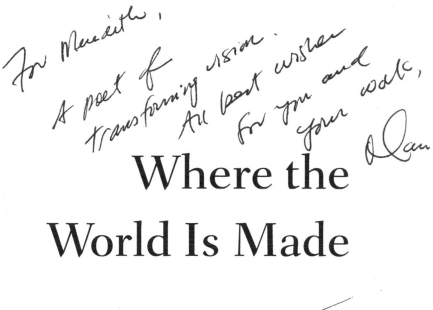

For Meredith,
A poet of transforming vision.
All best wishes for you and your work,
Dan

Where the World Is Made

DANIEL TOBIN

A Middlebury / Bread Loaf Book

Published by University Press of New England

Hanover and London

Middlebury College Press

Published by University Press of New England, Hanover, NH 03755

© 1999 by Daniel Tobin

Printed in the United States of America 5 4 3 2 1

CIP appear at the end of the book

For Christine

Time is for man, not man for time.
—*The Cloud of Unknowing*

Divinity dwells under seal.
—EMILY DICKINSON

Contents

Where the World Is Made

THE CLOCK

Bored with plastic armies,
he climbs onto the parlor loveseat
and watches the wide expression of the clock.
He doesn't know what time is,
doesn't know how in no time
those numbers will fill his days
the way water fills a bath
into which an exhausted man
lowers himself, not wanting to rise.
Sun and moon gaze back at him
from the glaze of the silver frame,
each with a human face,
his own face mirrored there.
Look closer, his mother says,
and you can see the small hand move.
And he leans closer now, steadied
in her arms, the hand a winded runner
lapped on the track. That's hours,
she says, the big hand's minutes, the quick,
seconds. And the boy fingers the pivot
anchoring them, his touch
stirs with the machine.
I'm older now, and now, and now. The gears
start to tick through every room of that house.

ONE

THE SON'S BOOK

"Oh hours of childhood
when behind each shape more than the past appeared
and what streamed out before us was not the future."
—Rilke, "Fourth Duino Elegy"

I. The Worker

Father on his knees behind the house
lays the rose plants in their beds,
palms them before he covers each.

Inside, too, he finds work,
building at his bench in the cellar,
fixing any lost thing: a table and chairs,
a picture frame, the grotto
christened for the Virgin.

The boy loves his father's hands,
coarse-grained, furrowed like the garden.
When he cries at night
and the dark figure fills the room,
he suffers against his face
their rough warmth.

II. Washing, and a Game

His mother sings, washing his hair
in the kitchen sink,
white lather whirling
down the drain's black hole.

Later, in living room's terrain,
tucking blonde hair
under a blue kerchief, her face
is shadowed by houseplants.

Through his gunsight's tunnel
the boy takes dead
aim on his mother's heart.

III. Crosses

Christ in marble,
pillowy white,
outside the convent
in the cedar house.

Christ in wood
of the carved stations
framed on walls
of the parish chapel.

Christ in paint
below the altar dome,
his crown dripping blood,
his eyes raised to heaven.

Christ in bronze, Christ in glass.
To each he'd kneel
with his rote prayers,
with the fierce mystery.

Christ in the flesh:
his mother's rosary
pressed to her palm
as if to feel His pain.

IV. What He Finds Everywhere

Maggots in the eyeholes,
the body a bag of fur
collapsed into the earth:
a wet squirrel on the road
matted like a child's glove,
snapped spine showing through;
and that bird near his steps—
he throws it out back. "Dirty,"
he whispers, not knowing its name.

V. The Dresser

Treasure chest of childhood,
his father's oak dresser,
its linen-draped top
a clutter of cufflinks,
ledgers, old bills.
Inside, the shirts
a boy could try on,
their tails like skirts
below his scraped knees;
handkerchiefs enough
to fill a magician's coat;
war ribbons, a Legion cap;
in the deepest drawer

a book filled with pictures
of women, a gun
wrapped like an infant
in white cloth.

VI. *Surgery*

His mother holds his hand to the light
to see the splinter caught
beneath the finger's skin. She strikes
a match to cauterize the pin,
lifts a thin awning near the tip
to dig it free. The boy cries,
shouts to do it himself while his hand
wrenches, tries to pull away.
Sit still, she says, it's nothing.
The blood trails into the palm.

VII. *Skitching*

In winter, through streets slick
even after salt trucks come,
he runs from his house to the avenue
where cars, tires wrapped in chains,
clink like B-movie ghosts before they skid
to the light. Crouching,
he grips a bumper's underside,
glides along the ground for blocks
through kicked-up ice and the driver's shouts,
hands burning with cold through his gloves.

VIII. *The Belt*

Black, stretch-marked, notch-holes
worn to tearing, the belt hangs,
buckle down, from the closet door.

Roughhousing in his room, the boy
hears through his world the *crack*
of leather on itself: the belt
doubled-over in his father's hands.

A burst door, shouts, the belt
whips through air, through cloth pajamas
into flesh—a click cancels the light.

Nightprayers. Foghorns grope
from the harbor. A streetlamp hovers.
Welts blossom. The belt,
flat snake, sleeps on its nail.

IX. *Swamp*

A flash of light through trees
quickens him, tempts him
from the summer yard
to the wood, as if a stark
hand had gestured a path
through gorse, dead leaves,
carpets of moss, and he follows:
over rockwalls sprayed with lichen,
skunkweed, cedars, scuttled oaks,
the murmur growing louder, the flash
become a maze of waters,

slime-channels, archipelagos of fern.
Ankle-deep in muck, he imagines
what he'll find: flints, antlers, deer ribs,
that dog skull staring from the bank—
till he ignores the call back.

X. *Flight*

The boy no longer says goodnight,
no longer whispers Sacred Heart Bless
as he's tucked under covers,
his parents grown tired of his moods.

One night, he wakes
unable to move, unable to see,
and feels inside a sudden stirring
like birds before an earthquake—

then: the explosion . . .

Was it a dream? Only an unheard shout,
the fluency of wine in water,
a white streak across a white vault
of sky, unnameable . . .

XI. *Priest Mountain*

When the late snows melt
and a few early crocuses
blossom sides of ditchbacks,
he hikes up Priest Mountain,
past shacks of the poor

and Klansmen's homes,
past the black bear's cave
and goshawk's nest,
till he finds a steep path
through broken woods, the cropped
granite and scrub-pine
when he reaches the summit.
And he thinks he knows
what Joshua must have known
gazing over the last crag
into Canaan, the Jordan
rising below him, the whole
valley filled with light.

XII. *Calvary's Tree*

For nearly a month in spring,
dogwoods bloom, almond-white,
as if to gather
the dead snow of winter
to a dream of flesh.

Soon, each blood-daubed
petal falls
to the street, is swept away.

XIII. *First Love*

Above them, tall gray stalks
rustle in evening wind,
thick beards of cornsilk
drooping from the husks.

He takes an ear, pulls
down its dried wash
till kernels show yellow.
A boar's tooth dangles
from his gold neck chain.

Making their way back
to the road, good shoes
reddened by the field's
bare clay, he breaks
a pigweed berry from brush
where the bikes lay:
its sticky dye bursts
between his fingers.

XIV. The Glen

Roots entwined
like lovers' arms.
Slate ledges
worn by water
over stone.
Shallow wells
where rapids calm.
Here, he finds the pull
of what's possible,
diving without fear
into the hollow beneath the falls,
rising unburdened;
sliding down the long slide
curved smooth as the small
of a woman's back
into the clear wide pool.

XV. His Mansion

Straddling the high stone wall that rises
abruptly from the street to the mansion
overlooking the bay, he finds his way
to where someone cut a passage
through the cankered fence at its crest,
through a garden's brittle hedge, its beds
of broken bottles where night-drunks bloom.
From there he sees trawlers heave into narrows,
above them the bridge vaulting towers
through which passes an endless thread of cars.
But climbing down, it's the same docks,
battered facades of homes. Raw brick. Cement.
The fish smell drifting from waves.

XVI. The Incinerator

Each night with a clean tug,
his father frees
the bruised garbage bag
from its bin, hands it
to his son to carry.

In the lightless hall,
alone, he brings his hand
to the latch, hears
as the door opens

wind sucked down,
the bag like fingers of the desperate
scraping the chute
as it falls.

Each week, the Super
ignites the waste,
and from that burning
ashes ascend.

XVII. Covenant

In the clumsiness
of hands, an eternity
of flesh . . .

The boy sleeps beside her,
her breasts uncradled
in an empty house.

XVIII. Necessity

There's no choice,
she said, and he
agreed. And what
was not a child
yet, but a minnow
swimming into its life,
they gave to the nets.
He woke then,
pacing the tarmac
outside the clinic,
to the textures, each thing
in its own doomed orbit,
as she turned from him
to go in alone.

XIX. Nativity

You'll help your father with the tree?
He climbs the clattery ladder
to the closet's highest shelf;
one by one lowers crates
filled with lights, balls—the store
of twenty Christmasses—into his father's arms;
passes down the draggled spruce,
its quills smelling of the year's must.

Together, they set it in its place
beside the window, drape the lights,
the garland, hang the balls,
fix the crowning star.

Lovely, his mother says, as he arranges
the crèche: shepherds, kings, Mary, Joseph,
the beasts with back-turned heads,
each dulled figure chipped—
the child, too big for the manger,
already cast in his prophet's stare,
arms outstretched, missing the right hand.

XX. Leavetaking

There's no road
in the dream he dreams
of himself as his father
working in the garden,
himself as his mother
nursing the child
who will be murdered

by Herods.
      On his back,
all he is: earth
that will someday lift him
into dust.

TWO

RENE RILKE

. . . everything is womb.

Before Orpheus grew, a tree in your ear;
before angels terrified you into song;
before *Rainer*, you were *Rene*, the dress
blue as Mary's robes, blue of the mother,
your collar frilled under its weight of curls.
You were all she wanted you to be,

playing dolls behind the black screen painted
with dragons, under your family's cross.
And they come alive in your hands: father,
mother, all the griefs received like toys,
until you lose the bliss of one who stays
forever in the womb. But weren't griefs there,

too, palpable as shared blood? And the fears.
From all you'll become you'll glance back
to discover who you are, for one purpose:
to be born again out of yourself:
doting girl, bitter cadet. A friend dies
in childbirth and she has your own face.

Born to death like a star to its constellation,
you will learn to leave the given name behind—
Everything is womb. Now you rise in the light
of a Prague parlor, *puer*, to prayers,
to a woman's voice calling the length
of the long hallway, and never turn back.

FIRST MEMORY

The afternoon sun slices through blinds.
You lie on the table, waiting to be changed,
your mother's face bathed in light above you,
nearly as beautiful as the one you'll gaze at
through the dead hours of childhood:
a schoolgirl, her strawberry blonde hair
tied with bows, fixed in the family album.

She draws her face so close, you can feel her breath;
her fingers strip the soiled cloth,
and she washes you shamelessly
in a time without shame.

It's not long before that face contorts,
before her raw voice grates your ears: *If I die,
it's your fault*. What boy
wouldn't long to know that schoolgirl
as he pulled his mother from the floor,
too drunk to stand, undressed her, put her to bed?

Once she told you how her brother died
of a clot that grew like a thought in his brain,
and her mother shipped her to strangers,
though she was five, and he was her best friend.
Gretel without Hansel, she waited till her mother
came for her, changed, bitter as the woodcutter's wife
who abandoned her children in the forest—
that woman rubbed your back when you were sick.

And her father—his hand still grips yours
from a nursing home bed—he'd crack his strap
against his children's skin, the taut flesh
snapping at its fall, and, who knows,
might have slipped one night into his daughter's room,
his wife turning over in their bed from a dream. . . .

In your first memory, your mother's face draws near,
and the child you were unclutches his fists;
but who is that other, crouched beside the oven,
teeth bared to a sharp grin, stoking the fire?

THE FARMER

I'd hear his shuffled shoes echo in the hush
of the apartment house hall as he made
for the stairs with their wobbly rail and spindles,
their scuffed marble, and would ask my mother
to lift me to the peep-hole in our door
that bulged like a cyclop's eye
to see his grim face under the pulled-down cap
before he turned for the flight, for his rooms
above our own, his whole visage shadowed
in dim fluorescence. We called him "The Farmer,"
but who would call that spare plot of courtyard
he tended a farm, its scraggly tomato stalks
twined on crooked sticks, waking from their patch
of uncemented dirt? Everyone whispered behind him,
a troll I'd watch through fire-escape bars,
T-shirted and unshaven, grubbing the packed ground
with his trowel, or fencing in the plants
with splints and wire. I never went near them.
Once, tossing a ball in the hallway, I felt
his soiled hand brush gently against my head
to move me aside, saw his eyes training down,
owl-like, a nest of hairs in his nose, and bolted
for our door. I was five when he died.
The men carried the bag down, a huge black cocoon.
In the yard, the few green tomatoes bulged under leaves.

WEASEL KANE

Once, neither of us more than five,
he tried to poke my eye out for no reason.
The teachers called him "bold," "brazen,"
his tantrums rattling placid Sister Allan:
"Patrick, you were named for a great saint,
try to be more like him. God writes
our true names in heaven's book, in our hearts."
I never knew who renamed him for an animal
so cunning and cruel, but the name
stuck like skin—Weasel, little general
of the neighborhood gang I longed to belong to,
and did for a time, squaring my shoulders
for afterschool raids on Woolworth's or Century's.
I loved our dimestore breaches of law,
or breaking back windows of houses
on blocks strategically far from our own.
I watched him grow through grades barking
curses at recess, his voice already tinged
with smoker's cough; or laughing, while his quick
fists smashed some new boy's glasses,
the smaller body pinned under his own.
Even the grackle-gowned nuns were afraid of him.
Patrick, it's ten years since that night
when you pistol-whipped a cop,
twenty since I saw you on the street, a day
you'd have had us snatch a woman's purse,
your hand at my throat instead, your eyes
flashing knives for the one of your charge
who from weakness, fear, or luck,
this time refused to follow.

SHALE PIT

Brandishing his cocked BB gun
Ogar shouts from the apple fort.
I crouch behind the wrecked Malibu
grown over with brittle sumac,
my own gun tight against my chest.
Beside me, Sanita kicks the shale.
BBs hail the rusted hood. Laughter
bursts from the ridge. *We got the fort*
come take it. It's Boone's voice, edged
with the same bravado that years
later will get him killed. *Stay here,*
I'll circle behind. When I head
for the sloped wall, a barrage
of mimicked machine-gun fire
starts sparrows from the trees.
Shale clicks under my Cons,
slips beneath, as I scale the ledge
shaded by oaks, duck into thicket.
Now, below me, I see the whole pit:
ditched wrecks, couches, exhumed trash,
Sanita cursing from behind the car,
Boone and Ogar drunk with conquest,
having raised themselves briefly
above the barroom dreams of their parents.
And the shale glitters in sunlight,
as if earth were a shattered mirror
whose splinters caught the sky, shards
of the lives to which we'll turn
when there is nothing.

MY UNCLE'S WATCH

"Bist du Jude? Bist du Jude?" the SS
officer repeated, like a schoolteacher
menacing a slow pupil, the camp for POWs
a train ride from Dachau. "Nicht Jude,"
my uncle told him: "I'm not a Jew,"
his whole body braced while the cold eyes
probed the face of the watch he bought
on Hester Street before the war,
the jeweler's name still etched on the case
behind the steadily turning hands.

Christmas, my eleventh year, a quarter century later,
I watched his unbroken body
ease into the big Queen Anne chair
in my parents' house, the family crowded round,
the creche a tattered barracks under the tree.
He told how his captor twisted the watch
once around his finger,
then tossed it lightly in his lap,
an act, I know now, of unbounded mercy,
given Himmler's boast—"I say who is a Jew."

That was the year of the other impossibilities:
men walking on the moon, my team winning the pennant,
the bishop's question weighing on me like a threat
before my Confirmation. Come Easter,
the tall nun would enter the classroom,
black gown trailing to her nobbled shoes,
her face framed like a mask
inside the peaked hood, and fire another:
"Who of you would give yourselves as ransom
for the rest if the Nazis came here now?"

No one answered, regimented behind our desks.
But I heard my friends' jeers of "Christ-killer" explode
from the schoolyard to the synagogue across the street,
the nuns' veiled slurs, the neighbors' brusque "Cheap as a Jew,"
and saw myself a little Jew-Christ marched alone
to the gas chamber—Christ of the ashen-haired comforter,
Christ of the lampshade—forgetting that God
is no hero, but a child for whom others are killed,
so my uncle's watch could tick on his unslashed wrist
in time without end and without redemption.

AMERICAN LEGION

My father called bingo, bartended weekends
at Bay Ridge Post One Fifty Seven
where he served stiff drinks to fellow veterans
who'd down shots and get bombed.
For years I'd go with him Sundays after Mass,
and Father McEvoy's homilies—
"The Lord is our Captain on the Ship of Faith,"
bellowed like an admiral to his non-coms:
then it was off to the Post with its forty-foot bar,
its quarter-slot pool table and formation yard.

Memorial Day, 1968; the men assembled
in royal blue uniforms of the Forty-and-Eight
(they'd kept the name, though we added two states):
black knickers-high boots, white minstrels' gloves,
gold air raid helmets cramped under their arms;
and among the crowd, my brother and I
waiting for inspection before the parade
with the other Sons of the Legion—
"What's your name?" "Tobin, sir,"
my voice snapping to the command
the way the possessed boy answered Jesus.

    * * *

At attention, I can see my father's friends:
Old Charlie Kerr, gassed voiceless in a trench
in the First War, the Post's mascot and janitor,
with a bald eagle face and nasal rasp,
in each ear a hearing aid tuned to the past;
and beside him, Cliff Jensen, who marched with a limp

and fingered the shrapnel we jostled to see,
collapsing to the floor, grabbing our knees,
as if we'd been hit by flak ourselves.
A Purple Heart at the Battle of the Bulge,
the story went. And strutting through the yard,
Commander Ed Meyer, ex-sergeant, Korea,
hair cropped to his forehead in a balding "V,"
signalling his troops to assume their ranks.
Frank Dillon, Sylvester Devlin, Eddie Caravone . . .

    * * *

My father's medals hung on the foyer wall,
pinned on black velvet behind gilt-framed glass
next to his past commander's picture
and a plaque dedicated to "Our Lady of the House"
who'd bless everyone who went in and out.
One night, the death-rolls over on the News,
I heard Bobby Carney, back from Vietnam,
say in the kitchen, "Those gooks'll do anything."
Almost daily I'd root through the family hope chest,
under albums, letters, my mother's wedding dress,
to find the gun, a German lugar, and fire
mouthed shots into my brother's head;
or would stare at the photo from the Philippines:
a corpse splayed on the troubled bamboo reeds
in black and white, the eyes shocked open,
his blood a billowed cloud on the shredded shirt.
On the back: *Leyte Gulf, dead Jap clipped in battle.*

    * * *

In the snapshot taken that Memorial Day,
my brother and I salute the camera

in our new gray uniforms, emblazoned ties,
our numbered caps cocked on our crewcuts,
while the Post's flagpole rises behind us
and the monument draped in purple.
Our father's shadow spills at our feet
as if something had stained the gravel.

When I'd watch the News, the bags returned
like trash shipped from the Fresh Kills dump:
twenty-one guns aimed at the sky
and an unknown soldier for the unburied.
Another war was passing by, and I,
ardent for some desperate glory,
took pot-shots with a plastic gun.
If my dead come back to ask me why,
I'll tell them my name is Legion.

* * *

Some nights I dream the parade starts up.
My father and his dead friends in uniform
march down Bay Ridge Avenue, drums thundering,
their paste-on ribbons fading in the sun.
And I'm there behind, brandishing my gun,
drunk with war's dress while crowds salute
and bombers drone through the ashen air.
Down the hill we march, past gutted homes
through blown-open gates of parade grounds,
tracer missiles screeching over our heads
and across the deserted Parkway, its dead cars
clogging the artery, our commander calls us on,
over the rotted boards of the Ferry Dock
into the Narrows, file after file, under the waves.

A CENTENARY

(Maplewood Graveyard, Charlottesville)

Among the gapped, moss-sunken slabs
of this Confederate cemetery
where the trucks of Route 20
tousle yews beyond its rusted pickets,
an elaborate obelisk stands, the tallest marker,
whose name in Roman scrollwork makes me laugh:
Hottop, Adalbert Finke, born 1888, died 1899—
"Suffer the little children to come unto me."

Were he born seventy years later
to my childhood's gray streets
and not these lush Virginia hills,
he might have lived beyond eleven, as I lived
past my days of emergency rooms and oxygen tents,
the attacks growing fewer with shots and technology.
He might have watched, as I watched,
planes with their cargo of body bags
on the TV news, documentaries of The World at War,
the spindly white bodies like mannequins
bulldozed into their mass graves;
or maybe learned the word "genocide"
from a Time-Life history of the twentieth century,
slowly waking, as his parents hoped, "to a knowledge
of the world," as he tried to learn compassion.

None of it would have done him much good
when my friends and I corralled him down the block,
or in the dark part of the schoolyard behind the handball wall
the monitoring nuns couldn't see behind.

There, we'd have mocked him till someone smashed his
    glasses,
or one of us, whose conscience suddenly woke,
let him break through the vicious ring
to run weeping home. How many of us were caught
in that circle, saw those faces contorted
with timeless cruelty, and took his place among them?

As it is, I picture him in some big parlor chair
on his father's lap, listening to stories of the Civil War;
or in bed, his mother's hand wiping his forehead
as he spits slick blood into a cup.
Maybe, before his lungs collapsed to useless sacks,
he was the brat springing from behind doors
to scare the maids and nurses, being groomed
in the town for a minor greatness.
This garish monument marks that hope.

Now, crows gather in the live oak
that shades his grave. It must be hard to see them
through the dirt and clumped grass of himself,
to see oak limbs raising themselves toward the sky,
to see the plane's vapor trail skirting the emptiness,
to see my face, so much nearer. Dead child,
would you have been a good man? I leave you to the ground,
to the crumbling walls and thriving green.

HANGING CURTAINS

I hold the bare rod, a vaulting pole
in my hands, its tarnished bronze
smoky in windowlight, then slide apart
the fitted halves, the blind inhering tunnels.
And my father counts the rings,
one for each curtain hook. He slips
them along the length, saying nothing.

His thick fingers that held the strap
taut, an inch from my eyes, then
snapped the folded leather in warning,
now fumble and resume.
I fit the two shafts into one again:
How old he's become, face raw,
his eyes ringed with disappointment.

Only in silence were we close,
long pauses filled by TV chatter,
or sports talk you hear in smoky rooms—
men huddled together, backslapping,
chinking glasses: as now we let our task
replace the risk of certain words, each of us
knowing what might be said is said too late.

So I climb the ladder, set the fixed pole
in its mounts, and thread
with my father's help each hook
through a ring's eye, link by link,
the heavy folds handed over,
drawn along the track,
more and more canceling the light.

NO ANGELS BUT OURSELVES

"What will become of us?" my uncle labors,
barely audible in the dull fluorescence
of Maimonides' lobby. Ten floors up,
my aunt's cancer's wasted her to sixty pounds.
I squeeze his hand, soft as a boy's, but raw,
let it fall limp against his side. The stroke's
knocked a chink in the wall between us, the way
I once dreamt light would glint on the faces
of souls on Judgment Day when we'd wake
from our dust like children from a nap,
stretching upwards, rubbing our eyes.
It's almost Yom Kippur, Day of Atonement.
Hasidim from Flatbush flood around us, like us,
waiting for the elevator, their beards
thick with the mystery of their God.
We are all here to make our visitations
before the night, no angels but ourselves,
smelling of the street and human sweat,
watching lit-up numbers descend, and parting
when the doors open to usher through the orderly
with his outrageous machine.

         I take my uncle's arm,
lead him through the crush until the lobby shuts
behind us and we rise, each floor distributing
the crowd to corridors of their own concern,
until it's only he and I stepping over the threshold.
Now it's my uncle who leads me, and I wonder
which is her room, watching as I pass families
hovering beside beds, the slippered feet
of someone at the edge, raising themselves,

the silent room with its curtains drawn, and then
her body almost taken by the sheet's confluence,
her skin so near the bone you could wash it off,
her face as I remember, but thinner,
ravished, asleep in the warm lap of morphine.
My uncle takes her hand, his eyes speaking
a question I have no words for, then rubs
her fingers, the i.v. jutting between knuckles,
looping its tube to the bag above with its clear
sustenance, its brined imitation of grace.
And I want to put aside the past's drunken rages,
the harassed wife embarrassed at gatherings,
her bruises puddling through the mask of rouge.

Outside, Greenwood's studded hill blooms
from concrete above duplicate homes, save
for the names scrawled under the bells.
Beyond, the harbor churns with traffic,
its Statue racked with scaffolding, the Narrows
bearing to Gravesend its cargo of silt.
Soon, others will come, her son, her sisters
and brothers. But my uncle will stay
long after the rest have gone, still
rubbing her hand as if to make a wish,
whether she wakes again or sleeps.

THREE

BOETHIUS IN DOWNSTATE

It's impossible to say why he keeps coming back,
so out of place in his consul's robes
torn and moth-eaten through centuries
of wandering what he called "this dull earth"—
tired old statesman, so far
from the burnish of eternal forms.
Now, like a lost boy stumbling on
an insistent path through some thick wood
he wakes to low moans, the beacon
of a television dazing the ward.
Here again are prisons where a man sits
in stained pajamas, cheeks sunken, spittle
glazing his stubbled chin; where a woman,
brain blighted like a walnut from within,
her housedress shredded by manic fingers,
stares as through the bars of her name.
The tube's glow throws a patina on their faces,
on the face of this philosopher who witnesses,
via satellite, the overthrow of the Good
in the fate of newsworthy refugees,
and the newest Goth mugs for the camera,
pats the head of the young hostage
whose parents, half a continent away,
must accept the sham as consolation. . . .
Pride, honor, power, fame, sweet husk
of the body: for him every desire
withers to chaff in the mind's vise.
"To be anything but what I am"—a crab
scuttling through primeval muck; a wolf
tearing at its prey; an earthworm, slow angel,
bearing the stunned flesh to resurrection.

"Divine Sophia, my physician, you who see
beginning and end, who judge why the fortunes
of evil men flourish like gardens nourished
on richest loam, wipe this cloud of mortal things
from my eyes." And once again, as long ago,
a pear tree blazes up at him, the wind
already alive with the scent of fruit
to be gathered, of the fruit that will fall.

AN EVENING

You hear upstairs a child screaming.
It's a bad dream these thuds and shouts,
screeches, wails battering the ceiling
that shields those shattered lives from yours.

A bad dream surely. Thuds and shouts
hammering through the atmosphere
that shields these shattered lives from yours,
and all that you can feel is fear

hammering through the atmosphere
you'd like to pull around yourself,
were there something else to feel but fear.
Inside, deep down, you sense a gulf

open that would pull you to itself,
a sun cracked to its core. Nothing
inside can make sense of that gulf,
or the gnawing chill when mothering

is a sun cracked to its core, nothing
soft, just a hard, relentless music
that gnaws. This chill when mothering
burns, gutters till the air is sick

with the hard, relentless music
of another's pain, is blue-black,
burning, guttering, the air sick,
the world a fist that lashes back

on itself in pain. O blue-black
the racket raised in the shadow-valley,
and the world a fist that lashes back.
Maybe it's the cat in the alley

you say (yourself in the valley)
those nights when love is past believing.
But there is no cat in the alley,
just the truth upstairs—that child, screaming.

A HUNGER

(Tuam, County Galway)

The farmer comes home late from the pub
his one evening free from work,
and finds what he feared, the heifer sick,
one hoof jutting from the straining rump,
the other turned back inside the womb—
as if the calf had lost its way,
nature itself unsure of the path.

It's no miracle, as he rolls his sleeve,
then plunges his arm, elbow deep, into the cow,
shifts the limb, a difficult gear, into place.
Now, he tightens the knotted rope around both,
and pulls until the shocked face emerges,
then spreads the opening wider, his hands
bristling with blood and water,
while the beast drones its low, unhuman cry.

Mastery is nothing but perfection of habit,
years on an unwanted farm, nursing cows,
nursing the mother who begged him to stay,
sentencing him to his blank inheritance,
until what tumbles into straw is an afterthought,
the moment spilling into its absence—
What I do is not done out of love;
in such loneliness I carry my dead.

Later, after the mother licks the new calf clean,
and it starts to hobble on its spindly legs,
he will guide it to the tit, the dumb mouth
sucking anything, even the bloody sac
that hangs deceptively behind the tail
and, if eaten, could kill.

A PASSION

Everyone loved him, not least
the women—demoiselles of the Sacred Heart—
who'd corner him at functions, whisper
"He's too handsome to be a priest";
and the husbands who saw him
as they saw themselves: good,
hard working, taking up the cross
of their slackened charms.

But it was the boy he loved, quiet,
troubled, chewing his fingers
in the school's bustling hallway
under the nuns' protective stare:
Jokes after lunch in the yard,
movies, evening visits to the rectory
for counsel, confession in the priest's room,
until he felt the man's hand
grace lightly on his thigh.

Without forgiveness there is no life,
by which Jesus meant life eternal,
present here and now as love—
the kingdom which is like a mustard seed.
The boy told what happened to no one,
grew older, until it drifted from him
the way silt sweeps under and is gone.

The young priest, transferred from parish
to parish, continued his rounds. And what each
kept in his heart weighed less than air
that when it gathers head will lift
anything to destroy the house.

A ROMANCE

As though a film were flicked on,
those two shuffle through a door
in my mind, ancient husband
and wife we met as we left
our year-long rental in Rome.

We'd been hauling the sea chest
we bought used on Viale
Regina Margherita
down the narrow flight to our
waiting taxi, the battered

straps fraying off the buckles,
both of us barely holding on.
They maneuvered to the side
of the tight entranceway, away
from our lugged trunk, the man

lifting his arm to shield her
whom he loved maybe from childhood.
He held her close beside
the terra cotta colored wall,
as if what we bore were more

dangerous than we knew: clothes,
books, our trove of souvenirs—
pieces of our separate lives
accrued to a common weight.
Handled badly, it could harm.

Or maybe they heard foreign shouts
nights from behind our door,
a pounded fist, when whole days
exploring the Forum, searching
for Berninis in alleyways,

were not enough to halt
our slow decline. We broke
like a fault running under earth:
a shaken house, shattered vase
until the city topples.

Maybe they wanted no part.
But why did the old man
hustle back, suddenly
graceful, to hold the door
a little more open

as we guided the heavy crate
tenderly between the jambs,
his wife stooped by the stairs,
gripping the banister? To be
rid of us? Or could he see

what we could not: indifference
gathering like a fine soot?
Grazie, we nodded, grazie,
as we carried it to the cab, then
heaved it into the back.

When we pulled into the traffic's
manic swell, I saw them
through double glass take the first
steps up the shadowed flight;
saw them somehow younger,

clutched in a café, or beside
the Fountain of Four Rivers
where all directions flow
from a single source, all
encompassing, and return—

as if the river we crossed
to the airport were not
the real, the Tiber,
its white levees glistening
with sewage, poisoned in its bed.

A FIELD OF BONES

    Bleached remnants of cow
the field gives back: scavenger, scavenger,
   turn them in the light—
                keyless ribs,
   flutes the wind tunes; a vertebra's puppet face,
hook-nosed, grinning; shoulder-blades
   like Chinese fans;
   jawbones that are narwhals, then seahorses
limning the Pacific; then long ships,
   mastless in storm,
   cribbing the straight-backed raiders.
Thread them together (the skull
   five tunnels of light)
   into a mobile
that clatters in every breeze.
                This is how the dead play,
   like children, when the flesh goes:
graceful Ariels, whose names are true
   because they have no names.

DEPARTURES

From chatter we pieced together the story:
how a man, maybe forty, parked his pickup
five hours down the line at Greensboro
and waited, who knows how long, for light
to slide at ninety along the rails
barely ahead of the grinding dark.
At the station, sleep still banded our eyes.
We'd unwrapped our bodies from the covers,
rushed from robes to hurl ourselves
into January cold, my bag manically packed
with last-minute urgencies—a jammed-in
sock caught in the zipper's teeth—
before we caught an announcement, not the train:
"Service delayed . . . a suicide on the tracks."
Who can say what drove him to the crossing?
I only know I held your hand
a little tighter those moments
while we waited out the early hours,
winter dawn rising gray as slate
in the station's sooted windows,
trees taking the cold like a medicine,
and was grateful for the choice we hadn't made,
long ago, in our separate lives: two knives
pressed to wrists in two bolted rooms,
guilt, grace, or something unspeakable
holding what made us hate ourselves at bay.

When the train finally came, its wheels
screeching down the platform, the engine
wiped of his trace, cracked ties splitting further
under its weight, I was thinking about grief,

how the least pain swells to pull us under.
On board, I rapped the glass once with my knuckle,
but couldn't find you amid the crush, then sat back,
feeling the lurch, and let the cold steel take me.

RETURN

Seven months away, I come home
to find you distant, mistrusting,
though it's nothing spoken, nothing
beyond a glance, the conversation lapsed,
or too planned, our laughter nervous,
as if what was learned over time
had to be more quickly learned again:
self-forgetting, the body's ease with another.

It's not wrong to want to rush, to want
to erase absence so love can rise,
an invisible ink, to our lives' surface.
But it's fear I feel now when I hold you:
my arms tight around your shoulders,
the words *I love you* choked in your throat,
desire a wave that takes the child under—
sudden, brutal—leaving only grief in its wake.

Every seven years the body's reborn, each cell
rises like Lazarus from its tomb, so the heart
derives a lesson: how love persists through changes,
even death. But might it not mean loss, touch
saying what the heart cannot—*you're a stranger to me?*
Tonight we lie together, trying to return to each other,
in darkness made visible by a little light—
stars that might be dead for a million years.

THE CHOSEN

1. *The Birthright*

> *"And Esau said, Behold I am at the point to die,*
> *and what profit shall this birthright do me?"*

Even in the womb I was stronger,
wrestling him till day broke,
and he gripped my heel, but I was first
to see light. So what did it matter
feeling alone all my childhood,
hearing our mother's voice grow softer
when she spoke to him, our father,
as always, silent as his God?

That day after the hunt, seeing
I could barely walk, hunger
a wolf tearing my gut, he ran
across the field calling "Brother,"
the sun risen behind him
so he looked a king, or god,
on a coin's gold disk, my skin seared
by light that cast him on the horizon.

Now, wandering these fields,
coming home after a kill, I wonder:
was it choice, fate, a final betrayal
that made me what I am? Sometimes
I wish I was never born to a world
where God's favor's won with a lie.
Then I curse my mother and her son,
the bitch land, and I curse the light.

2. The Blessing

*"And Isaac loved Esau because he did eat
of his venison. But Rebekah loved Jacob."*

For months my body
was a battlefield.

On my day, alone,
as I squatted beside a stream,
I knew God had betrayed me:
a horror, hairy as a dog
from head to foot.

Then I saw the perfect white hand
clutching the heel.

Why shouldn't the second
receive the blessing?
I could see
he was God's favorite
though I loved both my sons.

That day, my husband near death,
the one left to hunt
his father's supper,
and I told the other
Go slaughter a goat
and fix it for your father
and wear its pelt about your hands
and on the nape of your neck
and you shall get the blessing.

Why shouldn't he?
Was he not the chosen,
my Jacob, the beautiful?

3. *Father and Son*

> *"And Abraham took the wood of the burnt offering
> and laid it on Isaac his son . . ."*

Ahead, the mountain
jutted on the horizon,
a heap of spent stones,
jagged bone-pile.

All the way he was silent,
leading me up the path
like any goat or sheep.
Then: the altar,
dried run-offs of blood,
wing-flaps, everything below
picked clean.

Did he think as I lay there,
the pyre a temple around me,
his hand holding the knife to my throat,
I would cry out?

I sank into the stone.

So when the blade withdrew
and he raised me with his arms,
weeping, crying God's praises,
I felt nothing, being already
the given lamb.

Now my sons come to me
each for his blessing;
and they shall get their due,
older and younger
according to the law:
What is God but the place of choice,
the sharpened edge.

4. The Chosen

"And Jacob was left alone; and there wrestled
a man with him until the breaking of the day."

Dead sleep. Then light. My limbs
pulsing as if for battle.
Was he angel, man, or sphinx?
Wings beating deafened me.

I caught him by the heel,
dragged him down to earth: his robes
waves drenched in light,
his face pure light, obliterated.

Nightlong we wrestled, his touch
a sword through flesh,
until day broke on my stone pillow.
I rose then, my name become my dream.

* * * *

The Voice from the Ladder

Sometimes, when light
slants through a train of clouds,
and wind shudders through long
hours of night, someone will cry out
in loneliness or grief: *Lord!*
and may see us gathered there,
and may try to hold us,
or call others shouting
I saw God, heard God's voice,
and they will follow him,
though they have no knowledge
of our path through emptiness,
terrible, like houses of the dead.
We are only angels,
our wings beating furiously
against heaven's trap-door.

FOUR

SURVIVOR

This possum's got me backed
away from the trash can
where he's trapped, as though gods
too were scavengers and bite.

How starved he must have been
to peer into an empty pail, sniffing
only scraps of scraps. I lean
over with my light and see

the quick red eyes, the bared teeth
and snout, scragged fur, the nude
tail curled lewdly under,
his delicate blue-veined feet.

Once I saw one in a hedge at night
groping like a rat, and started
as I did just now, coming on
the unexpected. Another

I ran over in a hurry to be home,
the soft thump tumbling under me
old as dinosaurs, those tyrants
toppled in the comet's wake.

What nosed from the dust,
poking among What Was Left,
was too dumb to know
the power it possessed.

Close up this one looks
cowed, ready to die or strike,
like someone too long in want:
Some things survive,

this probably won't—*The last
will be made first*, Jesus said,
and *The poor will always be with you.*
There's nothing I can do

but tip the can lightly over and wait
for him to hunker out as if he had
a weight on his back, disappearing
down the driveway's rutted track.

BLUES

I, I, I, the stroke victim stammers,
the next word choked in his throat,
desire a ravenous animal
too crazed to capture its prey.

Calm down, his wife tells him, slow,
sitting beside him on the hospital bed,
tubes slung like puppet strings into his veins,
the loose gown stained with his needs.

But there's only I, subject without its verb,
its object, limp as his body,
the left eye drooped and tearing in its socket,
the dead hands motionless as meat.

Too young, she thinks, remembering his touch,
his arms hooping her from behind, drawing her close;
remembering the collapse, the long cry
of the ambulance hurtling him away.

In the room across the way, wheelchair
braced against the wall, someone searches
through static till he hears a voice
climbing the scales, each word

a crystal ready to crack, rising
in the stifled air: *Lord, gimme some lovin* . . .
Stiff lips play their stuttered I.
Fingers pluck the wheelchair spokes.

"THE WITHNESS OF THE BODY"

1. *Weightlifter*

Gravity's an iron bar loaded with rungs
he balances on his taut neck, thigh-thick,
wrapped in a towel. All he is grimaces
before the mirror as he starts his squat,
down and down, the Herculean belt
keeping the guts in place. Down then up
he works his near-buckling legs until,
from some pit inside, the barbaric yawp

announces he's done. Now he can linger
awhile with himself, his eye caressing
each increment of flesh: no longer like one
for whom living itself is a burden,
or the would-be saint prone under his weight
of air, for whom the spirit too is sweat.

2. *Radiator*

Crippled hosts of steam chink upwards
in choirs of screeching cars and hammer-bangs
brassy as bells from the squat cathedral
beside his bed, under a draughty window.
Waking alone is like this, the man curled
beneath the sheets in his own heat, a monk
who's missed his matins, the night's stale smells
still clinging to him, some noise disturbing
the procession of his dreams. How he'd like
to raze it from the floor, ruin of iron,

gross hump of inconstancy, but he knows,
as an old husband might of his broken wife,
this is it, the one almost warm thing in the house
whose irate babbling shakes him from his sleep
and into the brute plenitude of light.

PASSAGES

1. *Man Caught in a Black Hole*

What is this sudden travelling-through
as if a train had left the station
without a lurch, but full-throttle,
into the whir of absolute motion?

Surely it's no one's journey but my own,
quickened to thought from the womb's nest;
I arrived nowhere like weed to garden,
a fugitive passion to the breast.

When I shut my lids: galaxies, worlds,
the dust of a million creations
composed into that shining blur
glimpsed first as my mother's face.

Wherever this tunnel opens
there'll be a man with my own eyes
staring at me like a sun
waked from space, about to die.

2. *Stylite*

Let the faithful
laud me
where I sit
above them,
growing thinner
each year,
an arrow straining
for the mark.
To me they bring
meat, fruits,
food for this
unwanted body: all
I would leave.
To them I give
this image: a man
so touched by God
he has become
the ascended
column, ruined
finger the flesh
juts to heaven.
Each night
it is the one
wound I see
opening
between stars;
each day the sun's
empty face
burns away
more of my own.
I would assume

that gaze
as those below
assume mine.
Not the ideal's
pure form,
but the unbearable
light inside.

TREE OF KNOWLEDGE

*(photograph of a dismembered Salvadoran
rebel, Carpenter Center, 1982)*

Always in pictures of the myth, those two
stand under it, mannequins
about to come to consciousness,
the sexes hidden behind comical pods.
In Dürer's version, the woman
offers the bitten fruit to the man
who reaches for it, without thought,
like someone who knows he's already condemned;
while up the trunk the serpent coils
between them. So it was
even in my Children's Bible: hate
given shape under a puffy canopy
of leaves, the other tree nowhere in sight.

How different from this photo: limbs cut off,
the crowning fruit severed to hang, a threat,
in the town square; and where the sun fills the bay's calm
below the scorched edge of a hill: the savage trunk
rooted in ground, its bark bared to expose the spine.
And no one anywhere who'll tell the story,
but flies congregating on marrow, their children
quickened already—pale, larval shrouds.

BURYING THE CHILDREN

(Hart's Island, New York City)

We pile them up, box after box
the size of wine crates or incubators,
hauling them off the trucks, passing them on,
jotting the numbers as fast as we can,
400, 500, foreman keeping the ledger,
calling them out, we are piling them
in the hole. They are so light, these coffins,
they float along our hands, out of sight,
like toys, like lost thoughts, like nothing we know.
And if conscience could be weighed in pounds,
these are nothing: each one dead, each nameless.

But to stop briefly and feel the cold pine
against your palm—how heavy it becomes,
as if the dead one inside had begun to grow,
assuming the weight of its unlived life;
as if our souls began to suffer breath
and we ached for light: We are what we hold.

"THE NOTHING THAT IS"

1. Power of N

To be mathematicians
of the word:

Plato, for all his griping,
knew passion in the sunflower's
spirals; and who, but Pythagoras,
at Samos feasting on nuts,
knew better the shape
of bodies?
  In all things:
form. But in all things, too,
the power of N, breaking
form, shaking the shapes
beyond themselves.

Not quantity only, but density,
intensity—the petals
gone to dust, the bodies
to petals, and all, all
to emptiness. . . .
   And even the idiot,
his hand trembling toward the lit stove,
knows pain.

2. *Web*

Almost unseen, this world,
  its mythos scribed
   in feasted hulls,

begs speech, as though
  where nothing broods,
   a first word

bespoke itself,
  incipient descent,
   faint veil

spun out in cellar light,
  the spider's
   diamond heart.

IF YOU CUT YOUR FINGER, BANDAGE THE KNIFE

If you cut your finger, bandage the knife.
If you stub your toe, rub the wall.
If, stumbling on a stone, you crack your skull,
with your last breath ask pardon of the pavement
for its ignominy at your feet, for its grace
in waking you. When the murderer comes,
don't feel sorrow for his childhood, for the victim
at his feet; instead, take pity on the gun,
ill-used, like a mother, whose hard-hearted children
never come back. In the torture chamber, don't preach
to the torturers, nor comfort the exhausted broken ones;
but pray to the implements—rack, scalpel, electrode—
who know better than lovers the simplicity of touch.
Raise your eyes, kneel before the button.
And should you ask, *Of what am I certain?*
feel the wound, in front of you, opening in air
where the world is made, as in a womb.

STORM AND CALM

Like newsfootage of some faraway war,
a thunderhead charges over the ridge
at the town's far end—crack of gunfire
over trees, mortars thud a city.
The air shudders, bursts.
Whitewashed houses raze in the flash;
a veiled woman hustles her son
down a darkened alley.

No one should die here tonight, but somewhere
a tree's split to its roots, its bark
charred from the strike, the pulp
shocked white in a revelation of rain.
A few loose tiles whip from a roof.
Children watch from their window, wide-eyed,
waiting for the rest to shower down
like a flung pack of cards.

Soon, only a few drops splotch
the walkway's jigsaw of stones,
the sky a slow unravelling of clouds.
Everything begins to drink in light:
lawn, leaves, even the mottled garbage tins.
And the moon above it all, beginning to show
its human face—bright, impassive—
where the storm's passed over.

CAFÉ DU MONDE

Among name-tagged conventioneers, families
haggling portraits, random bluesmen,
palmreaders, tap dancers, mimes, garish masks
hung in a hundred shop windows
below the trellised balconies of a carnival world
we hoped to rest from, we found
the one free table. And there we were,
talking back lost years over café au lait
and beignets snowcapped with sugar in a city
foreign to us both. How quietly we slipped
into each other's histories, like fleurs de lis
in wrought iron. Those nights at O'Henry's,
The Plough, hashing out half-baked theodicies
over beers, had followed us. That tattered clown,
face powdered white, tying balloon poodles
for the passersby, he was your God of Mercy.
And Jackson's bronze statue above the Square?
It could have been the God of History glaring
beyond the Old Slave Exchange Restaurant,
the new aquarium and levee; buslines to Desire
and Elysian Fields, mules in tutus and straw hats,
drivers calling in Creole from buggies,
calling like the whores on Bourbon Street
to come taste this world, fleetingly, as it is.

As it is, I often feel like some lost soul
obsessed, blurting out my litany of names,
Royal, Ursuline, Dauphine, Vieux Carré;
as if, should I stop, each place would drift
down river, or sink in the muck of this sopped earth,
exposing its bones, every word dreaming itself flesh.

We are flesh who would make ourselves words.
That's why I like to think there's a substance
to this world, something the river keeps
in its passage to the Gulf, tributaries washed
in the blood of natives, missionaries,
scarring the crescent, shifting the land;
some sweetness that accrues like the residue
our waiter thought useless to wipe
from our table, after so many years,
conversations, lives, to which we lend our own.

FIVE

STATIONS

. . . you have made us for yourself, and our hearts
are restless until they find peace in you.
    —Augustine, *Confessions*

Bright wreathes, swatches of evergreen
laid at the feet of painted statues,
alcoves shimmering in candlelight.
Old women and schoolchildren
shuffle in the dark church
to their chosen altars:

Mary in her long blue gown;
Francis, his hand
perching a bird; the Holy Family.

I kneel before the Infant of Prague,
nearly my age, dressed
like a bishop—scarlet chasuble,
gold mitre and alb.

He points to his exposed heart
ringed with thorns,
topped with a blazing crown.
And the tall nun watches from behind,
clicking her chain of rosaries.

I slip my penny in the chute,
take from the cache of sand
the long wooden wand with its burnt end
to light from someone else's prayer
my extinguished flame.

* * *

These are the words of childhood:

Our Father, who art in heaven
recited, hands folded,
into pudgy cathedrals

of flesh, all of us
regimented in rows
boys left, girls right,
in the packed classroom,

chalk dust risen over sills
where the monitor smacked erasers,

whirling on panes
in burnished spears of light:

our uniformed chorus
silences traffic below

while your bride
Hail Mary, full of grace
decked in her black gown,

cross a silver brand on her breast,
ruler crooked under her arm,

searches the faces of her cowed charges
for the impenitent,
the insincere,

the ruler flashing.

* * *

Packed with parents, friends,
the church breathes
inside its stained glass,
the marble walls, ribbed vault,
accepting our host.

Boys and girls in separate lines,
we parade down the beaming aisle—
God's brides and bridegrooms,
having memorized the motions
that He might enter us.

Liturgy of the Word.
Liturgy of the Eucharist.

I watch through the ceremony's
long moments, ignoring
the two boys snickering behind.

All day we've fasted
to make ready the temples
of our bodies.

And I feel my own deep emptiness

as the priest breaks bread
with chrismed fingers, the host
risen above the altar, the chalice
beginning to shiver
into blood.

My hands part
thick curtains.
I kneel inside.
Black-out, door-shush:
Bless me father
for I have sinned,
the priest's face
a smudged stamp
behind the grill.
At his murmured questions
my sins surface
puzzled in the hush
of my breathing.
I absolve you
in the name of the Father,
Son, and Holy Spirit.
Now do your penance.
At the high altar,
under a saint's gaze,
my prayers rise, mingled
with candle smoke.
Leaving, my fingers
trouble a still pool
of holy water.
I emerge into light,
blinded, unrenewed.

* * *

Our mite boxes
jingle spare change.

All Lent
we give up pretzels
to save souls:
"pagan babies."

Starving where?
Bangladesh.
Ethiopia.

Can we find them
on the map?

So many colors,
the countries
of the world—

like flowers
in the convent garden:
Spain a red tulip,
England a yellow mum.

Outside the azalea hedge
whispering.

And dogwood,
its blooms
cruciform, stained
with Christ's blood . . .

Spring burgeons
to give birth again
to the Savior, the air
lush with signs.

Easter
we bring our offering
for the resurrection,
the poster-child's lips
consumed with flies and sores
below the altar:

O bleeding head so wounded
with crown of piercing thorns.

    * * *

Jesus is condemned
to death Jesus
takes up his cross
falls Jesus
sees his mother
the cross accepted
by Simon Cyrene
Veronica wipes
Jesus's face
Jesus is mocked
he is stripped
of his clothes
Jesus is nailed
to the cross Jesus
dies his body
laid in his mother's

lap Jesus placed
in the tomb—

     stations
that enrapt me
in their mystery,
my God
who has been forsaken.

    * * *

You will be soldiers
of Christ . . .

All winter we crammed
our catechism for fear
of the bishop's question,
pouring its dismissals
into our souls, knowing
what we didn't know
could shame us at the altar:
the absolute hand waving us
back from the rite of passage.

All winter, after school,
Bones, Weasel, and I
trespassed back of rowhouses
to grapple hand over hand
cables that stretched
pole to pole the length of blocks.
Below us, scraggy courts,
windows of cramped apartments
rose to view, brick facades,

backyards plotted with dirt
packed unyielding as cement.

How many times did we fall,
cursing and laughing,
cut on some untended shrub,
just missing the pickets?

When April came, and we marched
in scarlet gowns for the blessing,
we bore underneath the scars
of our passage, no questions asked,
the rote hand slapping us lightly,
turning us away to our separate lives.

    * * *

How many can I name?

Mike, Marty, Sean, Richie:
Hawkeye, Cro, Dexter, Stud.
Awkward Ronald
we called Moon Man.
Weasel and Bones.

With each new christening,
a new identity, a new legend—
Adam renaming the beasts,
banished from the garden
of memory.

    * * *

Water and chrism   you poured over me

through the priest's hands   and I cried out

so I'm told   like a child born

a second time   only my flesh was there

though the spirit hovered   over the unleavened soul

while the others renounced   the world in my name

suspending me   over the marble font

two weeks old   younger than Isaac

on the barren stone   the words your Word

trickling over me   over the loose bindings

white for innocence   white for emptiness

my slow chains   why wouldn't I scream?

   * * *

I place the faded green scapular
among the knick-knacks
on my shelf—driftwood,
deer's horn, cow's skull,
starfish, a myriad
of polished shells—
its sacred heart
hardly recognizable.

Below my window
the diverted creek
gurgles its fouled waters
through the black tube
under the avenue
with its endless hum
of cars.
    In the yard,
cocoons loose their army
of caterpillars to bring
death to the leaves.
And now a bee
crams its face, puffed
with lust of honey,
into the screen.

I am with them,
all the marvels
of this world,
all the terrors.

Notes

"The Son's Book": The poem's epigraph is from *The Selected Poetry of Rainer Maria Rilke*, translated by Stephen Mitchell, Random House, New York, 1982.

"Rene Rilke": The poem's details owe much to Donald Prater's biography of Rilke entitled *A Ringing Glass*. Both the epigraph and lines 9 and 10 derive from *The Selected Poetry of Rainer Maria Rilke*, translated by Stephen Mitchell, Random House, New York, 1982.

"No Angels But Ourselves" is for Kathleen Ruane, in memoriam.

"Boethius in Downstate": Born about 480 C.E., Boethius, the late Roman philosopher, poet, and statesman, was imprisoned and put to death for political reasons by the Gothic emperor, Theodoric. As Richard Green remarks, his *Consolation of Philosophy* "was one of the most popular and influential books in Western Europe from the time it was written. . . . The subject of the work is human happiness and the possibility of achieving it in the midst of suffering and disappointment." The poem imagines Boethius, who ultimately prized philosophy over poetry, in a different historical context. Downstate is a medical center in New York.

"A Hunger": The title alludes to Patrick Kavanagh's poem "The Great Hunger."

"Departures" and "Return" are for Christine Casson.

"The Chosen": See *Genesis*: 22–25.

"Survivor" is for Bill Wenthe.

"The Withness of the Body": The poem gets its title from a phrase of Alfred North Whitehead's used by Delmore Schwartz as epigraph to his poem "The Heavy Bear that Goes with Me."

"Stylite": is for Bill Thompson.

"The Nothing That Is": The title of this poem alludes to a phrase in Wallace Stevens's "The Snowman."

"If You Cut Your Finger, Bandage the Knife" is after a sculpture by Joseph Beuys.

"Café Du Monde" is for Joe Bessler.

"Stations" is for Bruce Beasley and Suzanne Paola.

Acknowledgements

My thanks to the editors of the following journals where these poems first appeared:

The Bellingham Review: "Departures"
The Beloit Poetry Journal: "First Memory"
The Bridge: "A Passion"
California State Poetry Quarterly: "Burying the Children"
Chattahoochee Review: "The Farmer"
Chelsea: "If You Cut Your Finger, Bandage the Knife"
The Cresset: "Web," "The Chosen," "The Son's Book" ("The Worker," "Washing, and a Game," "Crosses," "Flight," "Priest Mountain," "Calvary's Tree," "The Incinerator," "His Mansion," "Nativity," "Leavetaking")
The Cumberland Poetry Review: "An Evening" (under the title, "Pantoum"), "Boethius in Downstate"
The Graham House Review: "My Uncle's Watch"
The Hampden-Sydney Review: "The Clock"
The Literary Review: "American Legion"
The Marlboro Review: "Storm and Calm"
The Minnesota Review: "Tree of Knowledge"
The National Forum: "A Hunger"
The New Delta Review: "The Son's Book" ("The Belt," "What He Finds Everywhere"), "Blues"
Poetry: "Passages"
Resurgens: "Return"
Slant: "Café Du Monde"
Southern Humanities Review: "Rene Rilke"
Sou'wester: "A Romance"
Tar River Poetry: "Hanging Curtains"
The Tampa Review: "The Withness of the Body"
War and Literature: "A Centenary"
The Warren Wilson Review: "Shale-pit"
Witness: "No Angels But Ourselves"
Yarrow: "Power of N," "Survivor"

I want to thank the following for their helpful advice on many of these poems: Joan Aleshire, Bruce Beasley, Christine Casson, Nancy Hurrel-brinck, Tom Lux, Gregory Orr, Suzanne Paola, Michael Ryan, Bill Thompson, Ellen Bryant Voigt, and Bill Wenthe. I also want to thank Edward Hirsch for his encouragement, and the judges of "The Discovery/ *The Nation Award*" for 1995 and The National Endowment for the Arts for the aid of a fellowship in poetry.

"Man Caught in a Black Hole" and "Stylite" in "Passages" first appeared in the November, 1991 issue of *Poetry*, vol. 99, no. 2.

"Stations" first appeared in *Prairie Schooner*. Reprinted from *Prairie Schooner* by permission of the University of Nebraska Press. Copyright 1998 University of Nebraska Press.

UNIVERSITY PRESS OF NEW ENGLAND publishes books under its own imprint and is the publisher for Brandeis University Press, Dartmouth College, Middlebury College Press, University of New Hampshire, Tufts University, and Wesleyan University Press.

ABOUT THE AUTHOR

Daniel Tobin grew up in Brooklyn, New York, and presently teaches at Carthage College and at the School of the Art Institute of Chicago. His poetry has appeared in many journals, and his work has received several awards including "The Discovery/*The Nation* Award" and a Creative Writing Fellowship from the National Endowment for the Arts. He is also the author of *Passage to the Center: Imagination and the Sacred in the Poetry of Seamus Heaney.*

Library of Congress Cataloging-in-Publication Data
Tobin, Daniel.
Where the world is made : poems / by Daniel Tobin.
p.   cm. — (A Middlebury/Bread Loaf book)
"The Katharine Bakeless Nason literary publication prizes"—P. facing t.p.
ISBN 0–87451–935–7 (alk. paper). — ISBN 0–87451–956–X (pbl. : alk. paper)
I. title. II. Series.
PS3570.O289W47   1999
811'.54—dc21   99–21642